V13-10

JAN 13 2011

Volleyball

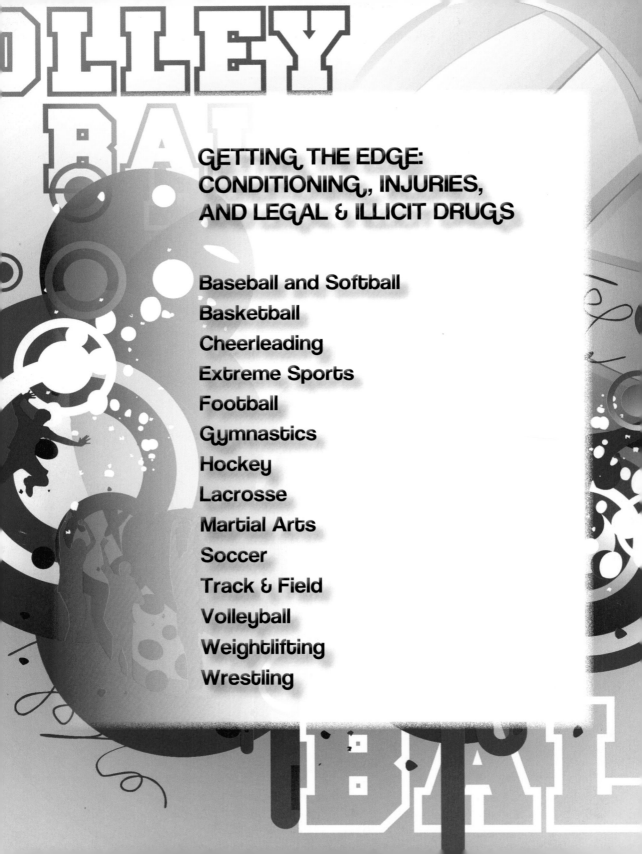

GETTING THE EDGE: CONDITIONING, INJURIES, AND LEGAL & ILLICIT DRUGS

Baseball and Softball

Basketball

Cheerleading

Extreme Sports

Football

Gymnastics

Hockey

Lacrosse

Martial Arts

Soccer

Track & Field

Volleyball

Weightlifting

Wrestling

Volleyball

by Gabrielle Vanderhoof

MC
PUBLISHERS

Mason Crest Publishers

MASON CREST PUBLISHERS INC.
370 Reed Road
Broomall, Pennsylvania 19008
(866)MCP-BOOK (toll free)
www.masoncrest.com

First Printing
9 8 7 6 5 4 3 2 1

Library of Congress Cataloging-in-Publication Data

Vanderhoof, Gabrielle.
  Volleyball / by Gabrielle Vanderhoof.
    p. cm. — (Getting the edge : conditioning, injuries, and legal & illicit drugs)
  Includes bibliographical references and index.
  ISBN 978-1-4222-1741-2   ISBN (series) 978-1-4222-1728-3
1. Volleyball—Juvenile literature. 2. Volleyball—Training—Juvenile litera-
ture. I. Title.
  GV1015.34.V36 2011
  796.325--dc22
                                2010016872

Produced by Harding House Publishing Service, Inc.
www.hardinghousepages.com
Interior Design by MK Bassett-Harvey.
Cover Design by Torque Advertising + Design.
Printed in the USA by Bang Printing.

The creators of this book have made every effort to provide accurate information, but it should not be used as a substitute for the help and services of trained professionals

Contents

Introduction

GETTING THE EDGE: CONDITIONING, INJURIES, AND LEGAL & ILLICIT DRUGS is a four-teen-volume series written for young people who are interested in learning about various sports and how to participate in them safely. Each volume examines the history of the sport and the rules of play; it also acts as a guide for prevention and treatment of injuries, and includes instruction on stretching, warming up, and strength training, all of which can help players avoid the most common musculoskeletal injuries. Each volume also includes tips on healthy nutrition for athletes, as well as information on the risks of using performance-enhancing drugs or other illegal substances. GETTING THE EDGE offers ways for readers to healthily and legally improve their performance and gain more enjoyment from playing sports. Young athletes will find these volumes informative and helpful in their pursuit of excellence.

Sports medicine professionals assigned to a sport with which they are not familiar can also benefit from this series. For example, a football ath-letic trainer may need to provide medical care for a local gymnastics meet. Although the emergency medical principles and action plan would remain the same, the athletic trainer could provide better care for the gymnasts after reading a simple overview of the principles of gymnastics in GETTING THE EDGE.

Although these books offer an overview, they are not intended to be comprehensive in the recognition and management of sports injuries. They should not replace the professional advice of a trainer, doctor, or nutrition-ist. The text helps the reader appreciate and gain awareness of the sport's history, standard training techniques, common injuries, dietary guidelines, and the dangers of using drugs to gain an advantage. Reference material and directed readings are provided for those who want to delve further into these subjects.

Written in a direct and easily accessible style, GETTING THE EDGE is an enjoyable series that will help young people learn about sports and sports medicine.

—*Susan Saliba, Ph.D., National Athletic Trainers' Association Education Council*

1
Overview of Volleyball

Understanding the Words

A **forearm pass** *is a pass made with the arms straight and hands together, by moving the shoulders to hit the ball just above the wrists.*

To **spike** *the ball is to make a powerful, high-speed attacking shot.*

A **dink** *is a soft-handed shot made with the fingertips.*

A **rotation** *is a one-position clockwise movement of players on a team; this allows each player to be in all different positions throughout the game.*

Substitution *is the replacement of one player with another for tactical or performance reasons; fifteen are allowed per game.*

The **NCAA** *is the abbreviation for the National Collegiate Athletic Association, the organization that establishes sports rules and regulations for colleges.*

History

Volleyball is a game played in over 130 countries. Indeed, the Fédération Internationale de Volleyball estimates that more than 800 million people around the world enjoy bumping, setting, and spiking at least once a week. Yet the world's most popular team sport is little more than 100 years old!

Today, in the United States, volleyball is played at least once a year by nearly 25 million people, making it one of the top-ten team sports. It is most popular among people who are twelve to seventeen years of age, with slightly more girls than boys taking part. Since the turn of the millennium, the sport has boosted its followers by nearly 20 percent.

Fun, fast, and growing, this successful game was born in the United States, in the state of Massachusetts. William G. Morgan (1870–1942) was studying as an undergraduate at the YMCA's Springfield College when he met James Naismith. In 1891, Naismith had invented basketball, and Morgan saw how much the game was enjoyed by the students. After graduation, Morgan took up the post of Director of Physical Education at the YMCA at Holyoke, Massachusetts. There he established a program of exercises, and his enthusiasm made his classes a great success. Still, he wanted more variety in his program, and for that he needed a team sport. Morgan thought back to how popular Naismith's game had been in Springfield, and he saw great potential in basketball. However, to broaden the range of people who could participate, Morgan needed a game that was a little less physically combative. So Morgan invented a game he called "mintonette." It required a range of physical and tactical skills, similar to basketball, but it was not as rough, and was therefore open to many more people. When inventing the rules of mintonette, Morgan took much of his inspiration from tennis and handball. Mintonette required a net 6 feet 6 inches (1.98 m) high; a court 50 by 25 feet (15.2 x 7.6 m), indoors ideally; and any number of players divided into two teams.

A match involved nine innings, with each team making three serves per inning. As in tennis, the server was allowed two serves to get the ball into the opposition court, and, after the ball had been successfully served, hitting the net meant a side-out (losing serve) or a point lost. Each team could pass the ball between themselves any number of times before hitting it into the opposition court.

The ball can be passed back and forth between members of the same team before being hit to the opposite court.

The sport caught on quickly—unlike the name mintonette. During a demonstration match at the Springfield YMCA in 1896, a spectator observed to Morgan that the aim of the game was to volley the ball over the net. Morgan changed the sport's name to volleyball, and its increasing popularity supported this change.

In 1900, after some years of competition, W.E. Day (a colleague of Morgan's) revised the rules. The height of the net was raised by 1 foot (30 cm) to 7 feet 6 inches (2.28 m), the number of players was limited to sixteen per team, and matches were now played to 21 points. But the most significant change was the introduction of a ball designed specifically for the sport. Volleyball's popularity soared in the United States, and then began to spread around the world.

The volleyball with which we are familiar today has its origins in the early years of the sport, before it was popularized around the world.

Volleyball Goes Worldwide

In 1906, the sport was played in Cuba after the U.S. army officer Agusto York arranged a match there. In 1908, it reached Japan in the hands of Hyozo Omori, a Springfield YMCA graduate. Max Exner and Howard Crokner took the sport to China in 1910. Elwood Brow, YMCA Director in Manila, introduced the sport in the Philippines, and within a few years, there were 5,000 courts throughout that country. In 1914, volleyball was drafted into the military when Dr. George J. Fisher, secretary of the YMCA War Office, introduced the game as part of a fitness program for the American armed forces. During World War I, both American and British servicemen played it, and its popularity spread throughout Europe and into Africa.

In 1922, the rule specifying three consecutive hits per team emerged. Later that year, the United States hosted the first national volleyball championship, contested by YMCA teams from all around the country. The game became truly international in 1935, when the first official international volleyball matches took place: the U.S.S.R. (the former Union of Soviet Socialist Republics) played Afghanistan in Tashkent and Moscow.

In April 1947, the sport's governing body, the Fédération Internationale de Volleyball (FIVB), was formed. The FIVB brought together fourteen national authorities under the leadership of France's Paul Libaud. Through harmonization of American and European rules, the court dimensions were defined as 59 feet by 29 feet 6 inches (18 x 9 m), with a net height of 7 feet 11 5/8 inches (2.43 m) for men and 7 feet 4 1/8 inches (2.24 m) for women— dimensions that still stand today.

World Championships

With a world governing body in place, volleyball became more organized globally. In 1948, Czechoslovakia won the first European championships, which were held in Rome. The following year, the U.S.S.R. won the first

Bence Bagics (in red) strikes the ball at a Hungarian National Championship Final volleyball game Kaposvar vs. Kecskemet, April 24, 2010 in Kaposvar, Hungary.

In June 2008, teams from the Dominican Republic and Poland competed in the World Grand Prix women's volleyball competition.

men's world championships, in Prague. In 1952, the women of the U.S.S.R. matched their men by winning the first women's world championship before a home crowd in Moscow.

Attendance at these early world championships was sparse, however, and it was not until 1956 that a truly comprehensive world-class event was hosted, in Paris. With the game now established as a genuinely international sport, volleyball took its first official steps onto the Olympic stage. Huge tactical steps forward were made as teams vied for gold: the forearm pass (bump), soft spike (dink), and defensive diving all developed during this time. In 1964, the first Olympic gold medals were won by the U.S.S.R. (the men's event) and Japan (the women's event). The sport has been a regular feature of the Olympics ever since.

Volleyball became increasingly popular with professional athletes. In 1990, the first Word League for men was formed, with a prize of $1 million for the winning nation. In 1992, this figure rose to $3 million; in 1996, $6 million. The Grand Prix, the World League for Women, was established in 1993.

The Volleyball Court

The court is divided into functional areas by lines at least 2 inches (5cm) wide. These areas are:

- boundary lines—two along the sides and two at each end, marking the playing area's extremities.
- center line—one across the middle of the court, below the net, splitting it into two team zones, both 29 feet 6 inches x 29 feet 6 inches (9 x 9 m).
- attack lines—these mark the front zones in each court and lie 9 feet 10 inches (3 m) from the centerline.
- service zone—this extends at least 6 feet 6 inches (2 m) and, at most, 29 feet 6 inches (9 m) behind the end line, and is limited laterally by two short extensions of the side boundary lines.

The Rules of Indoor Volleyball

Indoor volleyball is a game played by two teams of six players on a court bisected by a net. The aim is to use your hands and arms to send the ball over the net, grounding the ball in your opponent's court and avoiding the ball being grounded in your own. The back right player serves the ball over the net into the opponent's court, and the receiving team has three hits, not

Indoor volleyball is played by teams of six.

including blocks, to return the ball over the net. Players cannot hit the ball twice in succession, unless the first hit is a block.

The rally continues until the ball grounds or goes "out," landing beyond the lines that define the playing area. A rally also stops if the ball is not returned within three hits, or if one team commits a foul. Winning a rally means that the team receives a point and then serves again. If the serving team wins the rally, they receive a point and then serve again. If the receiving team wins the rally, they receive a point and the right to serve, and their team rotates one position clockwise.

Karch Kiraly is a prize-winning player of both indoor and beach volleyball.

Karch Kiraly

Karch Kiraly has been playing professional volleyball, both indoor and beach, for twenty years. Born in Jackson, Missouri, in 1960, Karch was still a young child when his father, Dr. Laszlo Kiraly, an immigrant from Hungary, moved the family to Santa Barbara, California. Karch played his first game of volleyball with his father when he was just six.

As an international player of the indoor game, Karch won gold medals in the 1984 and 1988 Olympic Games, gold in the 1985 World Cup, 1986 World Champions, and gold in the 1987 Pan American Games. After achieving everything there was to achieve in indoor volleyball, Karch moved onto the beach. He won the King of the Beach tournament from 1991–1993 and again in 1996.

Karch has won beach titles with twelve different players. From 1993–96, he and teammate Kent Steffes racked up seventy-six titles. With new teammate Adam Johnson, the success continued. In 1999, the pairing won the Chicago Open, and Kiraly's title record hit 140, making Kiraly the most successful beach volleyball player ever.

Lucilla Perrotta and Daniela Gattelli were members of the winning team at Italy's Beach Volley Championship in July 2008.

Volleyball matches are played over three or five games. Non-deciding games are played to 25 points, and the winning team must gain a clear two-point advantage (25–23, 26–24, 27–25). Deciding games (the third or the fifth) are played to 15 points, the winning team gaining a clear two-point advantage. There is no points cap in either case.

Beach Volleyball

The sport has never forgotten its roots—to promote fitness and fun—and in warmer climates, it was not long before a more acrobatic version of the game was being played on beaches. The earliest records show that beach volleyball was played at Santa Monica, between teams of six. By 1930, teams of two players were playing the sport, but it was not until 1948 that the first official tournament was held on the beach at Los Angeles. The prize was a case of Pepsi-Cola. In the 1950s, tournaments were played wherever there was a beach.

The California Beach Volleyball Association (CBVA) was set up to regulate the sport in 1956, and volleyball's obvious appeal attracted big-money sponsors. The FIVB was quick to formalize beach volleyball, featuring two-player teams, and the first world championships were held in 1987 in Brazil. In 1989, the beach volleyball World Series was established, and in 1996, beach volleyball made its Olympic debut.

The Rules of Beach Volleyball

Beach volleyball is, as you would expect, very similar to indoor volleyball, but there are a few key differences. The sport can be played competitively by two-, three-, four-, or six-player teams, same-sex or mixed, and only for a team of six players is rotation or position relevant. There are two formats for play. The first is a one-game match, which is won by the first team to reach 30 points with a two-point advantage. The second is won by the best of three games. The first two games are played to 21 points with a two-point advantage.

A block counts as a hit and each side is limited to three consecutive hits. The net should never be touched, and players may use any part of their body to play the ball, except at serve. There is also a play known as a joust, where two players both have their hands on the ball at the net.

The Court

Beach volleyball can be played on grass or sand, and the surfaces must be safe for players. For the two-player team game, the court is 52 ft 6 in x 26 ft 3 in (16 x 8 m), but for three-, four-, and six-player teams, the court is the same size as the indoor court. All have the same net height.

The Ball

This is the same as its indoor cousin except for the pressure. A beach volleyball must be inflated to 2.5–3.2 lb/in3 (175–255 g/cm^3).

Beach volleyball can be played on grass or sand courts. The beach volleyball net is at the same height as in indoor volleyball.

The Players

Players must know and observe the rules, and accept the referees' decisions as final, doing so in a sportsman-like way (although the team captain—and only the captain—may request clarification of a decision). Attempting to deceive officials or delay the game is not allowed. Players may talk to each other during the game, and coaches can direct from off court so long as they don't disturb or delay the match.

There are six player positions. Before each serve, each player must be stationary in her position. The service position (back right) is position one; front right, position two; front center, position three; front left, position four; back left, position five; and back center, position six. After the ball is served, players can move freely about the court.

After a team wins the right to serve, players rotate one position clockwise (one moves to six, two to one, three to two, and so on). The players' order is specified by the coach and agreed to by the match officials, and it cannot be changed unless it is by substitution.

Opportunities to Play Volleyball

Even a volleyball legend such as Karch Kiraly has to start somewhere, and the younger you start, the sooner you can develop your potential. If you enjoy playing the game, get yourself some equipment and a good coach, and see how far you can go.

As well as being a professional sport, volleyball is also a great way to stay in shape and have fun. It is played everywhere—in gyms, backyards, parks, schoolyards, on beaches—and it requires hardly any equipment. All you need is a round ball to begin, and you can even practice passing without a net.

Competing teams of two, three, four, or six players each can play beach volleyball, rather than the six it takes to make an indoor volleyball team.

STARTING OUT

U.S.A. Volleyball runs a Youth Program called the United States Youth Volleyball League (www.usyvl.com). This program welcomes boys and girls ages seven to fifteen, and teaches the importance of FAST: Fun—Action—Skills—Teamwork. Parents can volunteer to help out as coaches, assistants, first-aiders, and administrators. Only a few states, however, currently have leagues set up: Alaska, California, Florida, Illinois, Maryland, Nevada, New York, Pennsylvania, and Washington.

The original "King of the Beach," Sinjin Smith, and his teammate, Randy Stoklos, provide masterclass camps in beach volleyball for anyone eight years or older, at State Beach in Pacific Palisade, California. Karch Kiraly himself is associated with the Starlings Volleyball Club program, aimed at bringing the benefits of playing volleyball to girls ages nine and over from underprivileged backgrounds.

For those who decide that they want to play the sport seriously, rather than just have fun with it, most high schools have teams of some sort.

If you find that you are better than your teammates and most of the players that you compete against, you should nurture your talent by taking a summer camp course that is recognized by U.S.A. Volleyball. There you will receive coaching on technique, fitness, and nutrition, as well as have the opportunity to raise the standard of your performance by learning to play at a more advanced level. If your camp is affiliated with the U.S.A. Volleyball Talent Identification Program, your coach will be acting as a scout for U.S.A. Volleyball, identifying the best young talent in the country for special training. The coach will also have contacts with colleges throughout the country that are geared toward volleyball.

Most of America's top sports talent emerges from colleges where intensive courses develop talented youths into professional athletes. Attending college is expensive, and if you need financial assistance, there are many scholarships for which you can apply.

COLLEGE VOLLEYBALL

First, you need to find a college that specializes in volleyball. Most colleges offer such courses (www.collegeview.com/college/collegesearch), but certain colleges produce players of the highest caliber. The reputation of individual colleges rises and falls as coaches come and go, but there are some colleges that will always provide an environment that encourages excellence in this sport. Right now, the best such colleges are Stanford University, Penn State University, California State University (Long Beach), University of Hawaii, and University of California at Los Angeles (U.C.L.A.) for women; and Brigham Young University, Pepperdine University, U.C.L.A, Hawaii, and Penn State for men.

The country's best college teams compete for honors in the NCAA (National Collegiate Athletic Association) championships. The National coaches will select from this highest college level the players that they want to represent the country in the All-American team.

Players such as Lloyd Ball and Karch Kiraly are two of the finest athletes ever to represent their country. While not every volleyball player may go on to reach this elite level, there are many other options available, including numerous professional teams, an even greater number of regional teams, and hundreds of amateur teams. All these teams naturally need players, coaching staff, and support staff, so there are many opportunities for a career in volleyball—even if you are not Karch Kiraly!

2
Mental Preparation and Safety

Understanding the Words

Meditation *is a self-directed practice for relaxing the body and calming the mind.*

A **visualization** *is a mental picture.*

When the arch of the foot **overpronates**, *it collapses inward to an excessive degree when taking a step.*

A **floater** *is a serve hit with no follow-through or spin.*

The technique of **strapping** *an injured part of the body to limit the movement of a joint when returning to a sport after injury.*

Buddy taping *is strapping an injured finger to the uninjured finger next to it to prevent further injury and unnecessary movement.*

Your Mind's Role

In order to play your best in practice or a match, you must not only be in shape physically, but also mentally. Even if you have perfect technique and quick reflexes, these will do you no good if you don't have a positive attitude; it is important to be in a good frame of mind when playing, and try to be positive no matter how hard it might be.

There are many different methods for taking control of your mind and keeping your attitude in check. If you are not relaxed enough to concentrate fully on the game and your role on the team, you will be less effective as a player and more susceptible to injury. To control nerves and anxiety there are many different methods, so it's best to explore all the options and find what works for you. Some people listen to loud music to pump themselves up, others prefer deep breathing and relaxation, and some find that meditation helps them to clear their minds. Other techniques include stretching and yoga, which warm you up physically, and at the same time relax and prepare you mentally. Any of these methods will help lessen your anxiety about the game. They will help you focus on what is really important: your performance individually and as a team player.

Once you have released the anxiety that clouded your mind and prevented you from gaining focus, mentally rehearse to prepare for your performance. Think about your duties on the court and how you have been coached to play. Recall what you have done wrong and what steps you have taken to correct those mistakes. Think of the last time you performed well; what set that performance apart? What made the difference? That is what you need to succeed.

Picture yourself out on the court with your team. The more realistic your visualization, the more it will help you to mentally rehearse and feel comfortable when it comes time to perform. Imagine the roar of the crowd, the sound

Serving

Serving Underhand

- Stand facing the opposition court with the left foot forward.
- Hold the ball at waist height with the left hand and draw back the right arm. Simultaneously lean forward, placing your weight on your left foot, and swing the right arm toward the ball.
- Withdraw the left hand just before contact, hit the ball with the palm or heal of the right, then follow through with the right arm.

Serving Overhand

- Stand facing the opposition court with your left foot forward and the ball at chest level in your left hand. Raise and draw back your right arm.
- With your wrist stiff and your arm straight, toss the ball vertically 18–24 in (45–60 cm).
- Simultaneously lean forward, placing your weight on your left food, then swing the right arm forward to hit the ball with the heel of the right hand, and follow through.

Right-handed players will serve the ball overhand with their right hand, tossing it into the air with their left. Left-handed players may do the opposite.

of sneakers on the wooden floor, the feel of the volleyball soaring into the air as you strike it. Helping yourself become relaxed both physically and emotionally will improve your play by making you feel more at ease on the court.

Most of us, though, are guilty at times of getting a little too involved in our game. Sometimes the passion overpowers the play, and in our urge to spike the ball through the floor, we mess up. It is important for each of us to find our most productive level of energy, in terms of performance. We must have enough adrenaline flowing in our blood to sharpen our eyes, ears, and reactions, but not so much that we lose control. It is essential that we strike a balance between the will and the skill required to perform. That balance is different for every player, and only with practice and experience will you be able to tell where you need to be.

If you are too hyped up, your muscles will be tense, lacking their usual flexibility. Your coordination will not be as good as it should be, and you will be unable to focus your attention effectively. This means that you will be more prone to injuries, including muscle tears, sprains, and strains. If you lose a few points on the spin, it is especially important that you remain cool. Concentrate on getting the basics right, try to read your opponents' plays, and take charge. Above all, don't lose your head. If your fear of failure is too great, you will be too emotional to perform. If you and your teammates panic, you have already lost.

Improving Step by Step

While it would be unwise to beat yourself up over bad results such as losing a game, you should not ignore the experience either, or try to block it out. Instead try turning that negative experience into a positive one by looking at your performance and figuring out how you could do better next time. Ask your coach how you could improve your game and then, with your coach's guidance, create a training strategy to address the improvements you need to

Passing

Ready Passing Position

When preparing to receive the ball, stand with your feet spread, your knees bent, your hips over your ankles, your shoulders ahead of your knees, and your arms straight and at 90º to the torso.

Passing

Forearm pass, when receiving a serve; dig (the same maneuver, but defensively), when receiving an attack:

- Position yourself to meet the ball straight on, using shuffle-steps (sideways steps) to cover ground.
- As the ball approaches you, draw your hands together and move the arms from the shoulder, keeping them straight.
- Contact the ball at hip level, just above the wrists and with your hands together, then follow through.
- If you want to change the direction of your return, make sure your follow-through is in the direction you want the ball to go.

Practice passing with your teammates by standing in a circle and passing to each other. Give yourselves enough space to move to the ball.

This player is ready for a forearm pass.

make. This is not a difficult step to take, but it is the first, and a very important one.

Your strategy should be made up of medium-term goals that are attainable and measurable. If being out of shape is your problem, set a goal to improve your level of fitness within a month. Run 400 yards (365 m) , and record your time. Aim to reduce that time by a realistic margin, perhaps 3 to 5 percent, after a month's training. Do not push yourself too hard; setting a goal you cannot attain will only discourage you.

Members of U.S. Armed Forces Women's Volleyball team demonstrate the importance of blocking as they prevent the Italian player from scoring during the 3rd Military World Games held in Catania, Sicily.

Defense

Ready Defending Position

- Stand with your feet spread, knees bent, hips back, shoulders forward, and your hands ahead of you, palms facing up.
- Try to remain still while digging the ball, and aim to dig the ball in an arc of 20 feet (6.7 m) above the court, passing through the plane of the net cord about 3 feet (1 m) to your side of the net.

Blocking

Keep your feet planted, ready to jump, and shoulders square to the net.

- Keep your hands a ball's width apart, thumbs vertical, fingers diagonal, and arms straight.
- When timing your jump, watch the setter to find out where the ball is heading.

Once the hitter/spiker has been identified, watch his approach and see where his eyes are looking to indicate the direction of the hit. Then move to block it.

Once you have achieved a goal, raise the bar again. Your goal should be to become a complete player, equally good at serving, setting, spiking, blocking, bumping, dinking, and diving. You will enjoy the results, your game will certainly improve, and you will inspire your teammates to play at a higher level, too.

Equipment and Accessories for Safety: Indoor Volleyball

Like any sport, volleyball requires its players to have some basic equipment in order to play the game safely. For example, a good pair of shoes and kneepads are essential for the indoor game. For beach volleyball, a hat and sunscreen should be at the top of the list.

SHOES

A good pair of shoes is the first priority. The brand and model is not nearly as important as that the shoes are reasonably new and fit well.

Shoes age relatively slowly, so you may not notice the slight reduction in spring and support as the months slip by. Many players complaining of knee problems, however, buy new shoes and find their problems significantly reduced. Volleyball is a sport that places great demands on footwear: players need shoes that have a high-grip sole, and that can cope with take-offs, landings, and sudden changes of direction. All of these combine to shorten the life of a pair of volleyball shoes. Make sure that yours are up to the job.

ANKLE BRACES AND GUARDS

For volleyball players, ankles are the most frequently injured parts of the body because of the speed of the game and the amount of jumping involved. If you injure your ankles often, and find the injuries are getting increasingly serious and recovery is taking longer each time, you may need to use an ankle brace. (Do not tape strapping—it loses half its support after ten minutes.) You will also need to strengthen the ankle and increase its flexibility, but wearing an ankle brace will prevent the likelihood of further damage.

Wearing a brace also has a psychological benefit. The brace will make you more aware of your ankle's position in space, and you will find yourself moving in a way that is less likely to result in injury. The brace will also help you mentally: rather than worrying about your ankle, you will be able to concentrate on your role in the game.

KNEE AND ELBOW PADS

Volleyball should be played on wooden floors—a surface that provides at least some give—rather than on concrete or linoleum. By diving for a ball, you could easily damage a kneecap, hip, elbow, or shoulder, which could cause a great deal of pain and

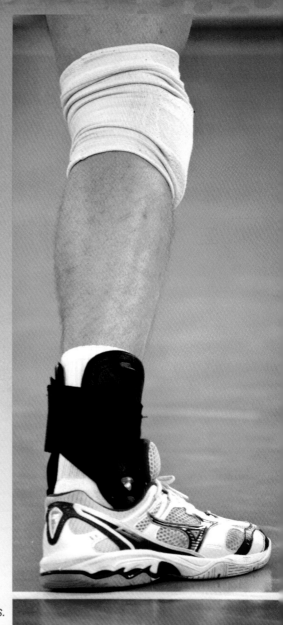

Volleyball players injure their ankles more than any other part of their body. Players may wear an ankle brace after being injured in order to strengthen their ankle while it heals.

keep you out of the game for months. Wearing pads will also help protect your joints against possible injuries during a fall.

KNEE BRACES, STRAPS, AND SLEEVES

Several products on the market are designed to offer support to the knee, but their effectiveness has not always been proven. There are several classifications:

• functional—giving additional support for injured knees;

• rehabilitative—limiting movement of the knee while it heals;

• prophylactic—for protection from traumatic impact;

• patellofemoral—helping the kneecap (patella) move smoothly over the knee joint.

Many players choose to wear knee pads to prevent injury, rather than wait until after they have been injured.

Arch Supports and Heel Cushions

If you find that you are experiencing knee problems, even with new shoes, you should ask about arch supports. If your feet tend toward overpronation and roll inward, your kneecap will not move smoothly in its groove. This is what causes much of the knee pain experienced by volleyball players. Arch supports correct overpronation and should ease any knee pain. If over-the-counter products do not help, consider having some custom-made.

Heel cushions are designed to help reduce compression throughout the leg during landing, but a good pair of shoes should give you all the shock absorption you need. If you do find yourself landing heavily on your heels during a game, work on building up your calves and improving your balance.

Of these, the functional and rehabilitative ones have been shown to be effective. Some people, however, believe that wearing braces may actually increase the likelihood of injury, either because this allows the athlete to overload a knee which is not strong enough to deal with the weight, or because the brace's external support structure serves to weaken the knee's own natural support structure. Most athletes who wear them, however, believe they help, and that factor alone is important.

If you do decide to wear a knee support, make sure it fits correctly; otherwise, it is worse than useless. Also, you need to wear it whenever you are

General Support

Volleyball played competitively provides a serious workout. Aches and pains are inevitable—although warming up and cooling down properly will keep them to a minimum. If you are feeling the effects of your workout, you may want to use some of the supports available in good sports stores.

Among the large variety available are Achilles tendon supports, hamstring supports, back supports, and elbow and shoulder supports. If you think that wearing one of these will make a difference in the way you feel and play, or if your coach has recommended you buy one, you should do so. Or you could adjust your training schedule and make sure it includes a little more strengthening work in those areas. The results will be longer lasting.

increasing the load on your knee, which means during warm-up just as much as when training or playing a match. Remember, too, that your knee brace is the least important aspect of preventing knee injury, or of rehabilitation after an injury. Stretching and strengthening the legs, and managing your fitness program correctly, are far more important.

FINGER AND WRIST PROTECTION

Injuries to the hands and wrists are the third most common type of injury after those to the ankle and knee—and you do not need a great deal of knowledge about volleyball to see why. Maneuvers such as the **floater** serve and

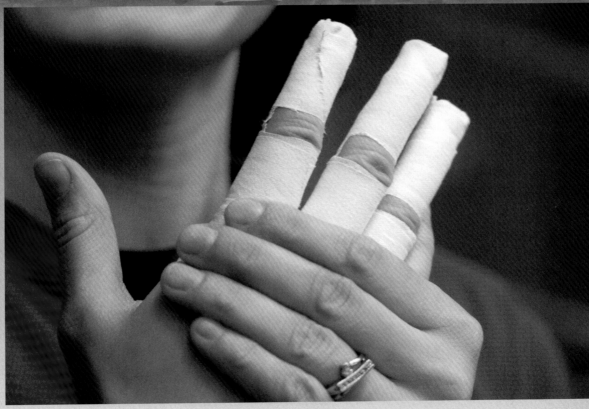

Taping injured fingers is often the best way to help them heal.

the spike place great amounts of pressure on the wrist, and throughout the course of a season, strains are not uncommon. Likewise, it is not unusual for fingers and thumbs to be sprained when blocking.

Gloves and other products are available to protect your hands, but **strapping**, applied correctly, will provide your fingers, thumbs, and wrists with the necessary support. If a finger is sprained, you can prevent further injury when training and playing by strapping it to the next finger—a procedure known as **buddy taping**. There are also finger braces on the market.

What People Are Saying About Volleyball

Volleyball is the sport through which I am able to express my God-given talents of being an athlete. It is a sport that involves relating, pushing, and encouraging your teammates. It has helped evolve me into the person I am today."
—David Beard

I don't really keep track of numbers. We don't even think about that stuff. That's not why we play. We play because we love it.

It takes a lot of hard work and dedication just like any other pro sport. Especially for beach volleyball you don't have to be tall or as fast as other sports. You just have to have the skills.
—Misty May Treanor

Extra discipline makes up for a lack of talent and a lack of discipline quickly siphons away extra talent, that's why it's frequently the most disciplined rather than the most gifted that rise to the top."
—Unknown

Safety Equipment for Beach Volleyball

Sand is a much more forgiving surface to play on than wood and eliminates the need for shoes, kneepads, and elbow pads. It also reduces—but does not eliminate—the likelihood of ankle and knee injuries. Even so, the outdoor game includes one big danger that does not factor into the indoor game—the sun.

SUNSCREEN

Even on cloudy days, the sun's UV (ultraviolet) rays are strong enough to burn the skin. For this reason, players, officials, and spectators need to wear a reliable, broad-spectrum sunscreen. Beach volleyball players spend a great deal of time on the sand, and failure to apply a protective layer of sunscreen will increase their risk of skin cancer.

HAT

Wearing a peaked, baseball-style hat will help to protect your face from the sun's UV rays. It will also help keep the sun out of your eyes.

SUNGLASSES

It can be very difficult to see the ball without a good pair of sunglasses. Without them, sunlight—whether directly, glinting off the ocean, or reflecting off something shiny—can leave you with temporary blind spots. Make sure your sunglasses are also UVA and UVB resistant. Eyes, like skin, can burn: if your eyes are exposed to sunlight for as little as six hours without protection, they will feel gritty and may begin to water profusely. These are symptoms of sun blindness, and the only cure is to keep your eyes cool and covered for eighteen hours.

FINGER AND WRIST PROTECTION

Beach volleyball players will find that their fingers, thumbs, and wrists take a battering. Strap or brace as you would for the indoor game.

3
Physical Preparation

Understanding the Words

Aerobic exercise is the type of exercise that demands increased oxygen, forcing the heart and breathing rates to increase. Aerobic exercise demands endurance, and requires the body to work for extensive periods of time, like running or going on a long bike ride.

Complementary exercises are ones that work muscle groups that work with one another, such as the biceps and triceps in the arms.

Reaction time is the amount of time it takes for the body to react to something; for example, if the ball flies over the net toward you, your reaction time is determined by how long it takes you to get into position to hit it back or pass the ball to a teammate.

Anaerobic activity is any physical exercise that is short and intense, such as weightlifting and sprinting. This type of exercise builds strength and needs less oxygen than aerobic exercise.

Warm Up

Just as the mind requires preparation to raise its performance level, so does the body. Unless you warm up or do some form of stretching exercise, sudden bursts of activity are likely to cause injury. Your muscles, ligaments, and tendons will not be flexible enough to endure strenuous physical activity.

A warm-up and cool-down routine is essential, both before and after exercise. It is a good habit to develop and, when combined with your mental preparation, provides you with a pre-game routine that will help you focus your mind on the challenge ahead.

The warm-up is designed to limber up the body and prepare it for prolonged exertion. Wear an extra layer of clothing to hold in the warmth you generate, and keep this layer on until you are called onto the court for the game.

The ideal warm-up routine includes three distinct aspects: aerobic, stretch, and practice.

AEROBIC

The goal here is to raise the heart and respiration rates slowly. As you begin to breathe more quickly and deeply, your lungs take in more air. This, combined with your increasing heart rate, raises the level of oxygen in the blood. This helps your body to convert stored energy and increases the flow of blood throughout the body. The increased heart rate also raises body temperature, warming and loosening the muscles and tendons.

Ten minutes of brisk walking or jogging will prepare your body, and it will also help you to clear your mind and focus on the game ahead. After this, try a few short on-the-spot sprints.

STRETCH

This section of the warm-up is designed to prepare your muscles, tendons, and ligaments for what lies ahead. While general stretches are important, be

Stretching is an important part of any warm-up exercise routine. In volleyball, a sport that involves a lot of jumping (causing stress on the lower body) and quick movement, stretching the legs is vital.

sure to also choose specific stretches that work on the muscle systems you are about to use the most. For volleyball, this means the shoulders, back, groin, legs, knees, and ankles.

Hold each stretch for thirty seconds before release. Stretch steadily and gradually; don't bounce or pump the stretch position, as this could snap a tendon or ligament. Slowly extend the stretch up to, but not beyond, the point where you feel it begin to pull. Work on complementary areas—for instance, stretch your quadriceps for thirty seconds and then stretch your hamstrings for thirty seconds. Stretch only as far as you comfortably can, and pay specific attention to areas that have recently recovered from injury.

PRACTICE

This section is designed to help your body and mind get into competition mode. You go through all the different maneuvers your body will be performing, beginning with the most gentle:

- Start with triangle passing, an exercise to raise your perception and coordination. It will also stretch and warm your shoulders and limber up your hips, knees, and ankles. Stand in a triangle with two other teammates, and pass the ball between you. Do this for three to five minutes.

- Next, spend three to five minutes serving and returning alternately in pairs—not at full intensity, but building toward match level.

- Then spend three to five minutes setting, hitting, and blocking, again building in intensity.

By this stage, you should be prepared for the match, both physically and mentally. If there is any part of your body that is not ready for what lies ahead, you will find out about it during this warm-up. If so, consult your coach about whether you can play.

Training Exercises

No matter what sport you're training for, there should always be specific body parts and techniques you focus on. For example, while certain hockey drills may be great to get you into shape and make you a better athlete, they won't do you very much good as a volleyball player. In volleyball, it is important to focus on your shoulders, hips, knees, and ankles, as these are the joints that receive the most wear and tear from performance. Also, learning how to improve your reaction time, muscle control, stability, and extension will lessen your chance of injury. It is important to focus on a number of types of training, including weight training, plyometrics, and cardio.

Volleyball player Kinga Kasprzak, a member of Poland's team, stretches before a match.

WEIGHT TRAINING

To train and strengthen your lower body, try these exercises:

- **Squats**: begin in a standing position, slowly bending the knees and hips until you are in a sitting position; hold for 10–15 seconds, stand up straight, and repeat. This exercise strengthens the muscles of the thighs, hips, and buttocks.

- **Leg press**: using a leg press under your coach or trainer's supervision, you can strengthen your entire lower body. Sitting below the sled, push it upward with your feet, and slowly lower back down until your knees are bent halfway, then extend again.

- **Deadlift**: Pull the barbell from the floor with both hands until your body is fully extended. Begin pushing from the heels, and bringing your hips forward, being careful not to pull with your lower back. This exercise strengthens the lower back, but can also cause serious injury, so be sure to work with a trainer to learn proper technique.

- **Bench step-ups**: Using just your body weight or holding lightweight dumbbells in each hand, stand in an upright position. Stand directly in front of a step bench that is 18–24 inches high. Place one foot (your lead foot) flat on the bench. With most of your weight on the heel of the lead foot, forcefully push off with the lead leg and assume a standing position with both feet on the bench. Repeat this exercise using the other leg as the lead leg.

For your upper body, your shoulders, biceps, triceps, and abdominals, using weights as well as body weight can be useful for strengthening. Incorporate these exercises into your routine:

- **Pullover**: This exercise will help strengthen most muscles in the upper body through a full range of motion, especially the shoulders, which are prone to injury. Pullovers improve the overhead motion used consistently by volleyball players. Hold the dumbbell close to your body and lie down carefully on your back on a bench. Bend your knees in a comfortable position, and hold the dumbbell vertically, with the farther end resting in your palms, and your arms straight out above your head. Lift your arms so they are right above your face, keeping your elbows straight, then slowly lower the arms back down. Perform 2–4 sets of 10–15 repetitions.

A leg press is a good way to strengthen your entire lower body.

- **Push press**: Grasp a barbell from the floor with an overhand grip, slightly wider than shoulder width. Position the bar chest high with your torso tight, and pull your head back. Dip your body by bending the knees, hips, and ankles slightly. Explosively drive upward with the legs, driving the barbell up off the shoulders and extending your arms overhead. This exercise strengthens your shoulders and prevents future injury.

- **Explosive pushups**: Start by getting into the pushup position, and lower yourself on the ground. Then, explosively push up so that your hands leave the ground. Catch your fall with your hands and immediately lower yourself into a pushup again and repeat, without allowing your chest, stomach, or thighs to touch the ground.

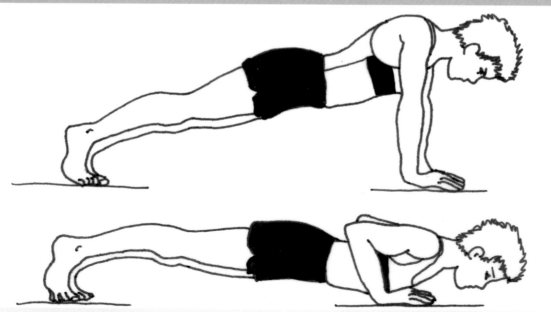

Explosive pushups build the muscles in your shoulders, which will help make your serve more powerful.

PLYOMETRICS

- **Depth jumps**: Stand on a box with your toes close to the edge. Step (don't jump) off the box and land on both feet. Immediately jump up and reach with both hands toward the ceiling, keeping your momentum from stepping down. Keep your time on the ground to a minimum, jumping right away once you touch the ground.

- **Over-the-back toss**: Stand with your feet slightly wider than hip-width apart. Have a partner or trainer stand about 10 yards behind you. Grasp a medicine ball and lower the body into a semi-squat position. Explode upward, extending the entire body, and throw the ball behind you as far as you can, generating power in your legs. Catch the ball on a bounce from your partner, and repeat.

- **Lateral high hop**: Stand to the left of a box and place your right foot on top of it. Push off the box using the right leg only and explode vertically as high as possible. Drive the arms forward and up for maximum height. Land with the opposite foot on the box, and repeat, alternating back and forth.

- **Squat throw from chest**: Stand with your feet slightly wider than hip-width apart and your knees slightly bent. Hold a medicine ball at chest level and squat down to a parallel position. Quickly explode up and jump as high as you can. As you start your jump, throw the ball as high as possible. Retrieve the ball and repeat the exercise.

CARDIO

Unlike sports such as basketball, soccer, or track, where an athlete has to move at a medium pace for an extended period of time, volleyball does not require quite as much endurance. Instead, volleyball players should be better at exerting quick, short bursts of power, which is known as **anaerobic** exercise. But a player must also be able to perform in a game without tiring.

Setting and Hitting

Setting

This sets up the ball for spiking and is also used as an overhand pass.

- Face the target with your left foot forward and your weight on the right foot, knees bent and feet spread.
- Raise your hands 6–8 inches ahead of your forehead as if cupping the ball, looking through the triangle made by your first fingers and thumbs, and keeping hands, forehead and hips in a line.
- Just before you contact the ball, straighten your arms and legs while keeping your eye on the ball, then follow through in the direction you want the ball to go.
- For setting, your goal is to drop the ball just inside the sideline, 3 feet to your side of the centerline.

- **Line drills**: Commonly known as suicide drills, this exercise helps to increase your endurance, but also focuses on short bursts of speed and energy. Beginning at the far end of a gym or sports field, your coach will set up evenly spaced distances along the length of the floor. Starting at the end, run to the first distance and immediately run back to your starting point. Without resting, turn around and run back in the opposite direction, but this time, run even further to the second distance, then return to the starting position. Continue this drill until you have run all the way to the other end of the floor and returned to the beginning, stopping at each distance along the way.

Hitting

This maneuver is used for attacking and spiking.

- If using a three- or four-step run-up, make sure your last step is the longest and most powerful. Plant your left foot, then swing both arms ahead of you and take off vertically with both feet slightly apart.
- Extend your left arm out ahead of you and draw the right arm back, above, and behind your shoulder with your right arm bent.
- Drop the shoulder and then, keeping the right arm slightly bent, use the heel or palm of the right hand to make contact with the ball immediately above and ahead of the forehead.

Cool-Down

After the match has finished, put on an extra layer of clothing so you do not cool down too fast, which would mean that your soft muscle tissue would become sore and stiff. Slow down your body by jogging gently for five minutes, then finish off with ten minutes of stretching, paying particular attention to the areas you have exerted most.

4

Common Injuries, Treatment, & Recovery

Understanding the Words

An **overuse injury** is an injury that results from repetitive physical maneuvers performed over a long period of time.

An **acute injury** is one that is caused by a single, traumatic event.

Inversion is an acute injury that usually results in a sprain, where the ankle rolls over the outside of the foot.

A **compression bandage** is one that holds a swollen joint or muscle tightly in place in order to reduce swelling.

Considering how fast-moving a sport volleyball is, injuries are surprisingly infrequent. At the Olympic level, a volleyball player will suffer an injury after an average of twenty-five hours on the court; at a national amateur level, after fifty hours. At this level, about half of all players can expect one injury during a season, though most injuries will be minor enough to allow resumed play within a week.

Jumping (or rather landing) in defense is responsible for most of the injuries seen in volleyball. Players have to jump when both attacking and defending. Blocking is also injurious as it can involve landing on the opposition's feet. Most hand injuries in volleyball are caused by blocking. The spike is the second most hazardous activity, placing the ankle at risk, and jumping places great demands on the knee. The more volleyball you play, the more likely it is that you will suffer from the single most common overuse injury: jumper's knee.

Broadly speaking, volleyball injuries fall into two categories: acute and overuse. An acute injury tends to be traumatic, caused by a single event such as a sprain, whereas overuse injuries become more of a problem as you spend more time on the court. Both these types of injury are most likely to occur to the ankles, knees, hands, and wrists, with the ankle being particularly vulnerable.

Acute Injuries

THE ANKLE

Ankle injuries account for almost two-thirds of all acute injuries in volleyball; most result from jumping at the net, either to block or to spike. If a player lands slightly off balance, or her foot moves below the net and lands on an opponent's foot, the ankle may roll over onto the outside of the foot. This is known as forced supination, or inversion, and results in overextension of the ligaments—usually called a sprained ankle.

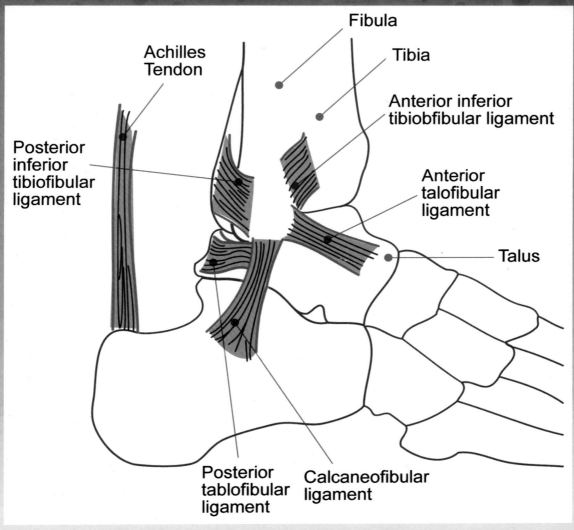

Fibula

Tibia

Anterior inferior tibiobfibular ligament

Achilles Tendon

Posterior inferior tibiofibular ligament

Anterior talofibular ligament

Talus

Posterior tablofibular ligament

Calcaneofibular ligament

Almost two out of every three acute injuries in volleyball are ankle injuries. The most common of these injuries is a sprained ankle, caused by rolling the ankle in a way that overextends the ligaments seen above.

There are three degrees of sprain. If the talo-fibular ligaments have been stretched or slightly torn, but you can stand on the ankle without too much pain, you will feel only a slight swelling and stiffness in the ankle. For second-degree sprains, the tearing of the talo-fibular ligaments will be more significant, causing heavy swelling and more pain, leaving the ankle itself unstable and feeling very stiff. Third-degree sprains involve the complete rupture of the talo-fibular ligaments, leaving the ankle disabled, severely swollen, and extremely painful.

HAND INJURIES

Most hand injuries are the result of blocking attacks. These result in sprains of the fingers and thumbs. Depending on the injury, a player will be able to go back on the court quickly, by either using buddy taping or thumb spica taping, where the thumb, wrist, and hand are taped for extra support. Sometimes, more severe injuries may require surgery, but these are unusual.

KNEE INJURIES

Acute injuries to the knee are rare because most players wear kneepads. Sometimes, severe twists can result in torn knee ligaments that require surgery, but far more common is the overuse injury often referred to as jumper's knee.

Overuse Injuries

KNEES

Jumper's knee is a dull, aching pain usually located at the bottom of the kneecap. Technically known as patellar tendonitis, it is responsible for 80 percent of overuse injuries in volleyball. The more often you jump, and the more powerfully you jump, the more likely you are to suffer from it. Studies

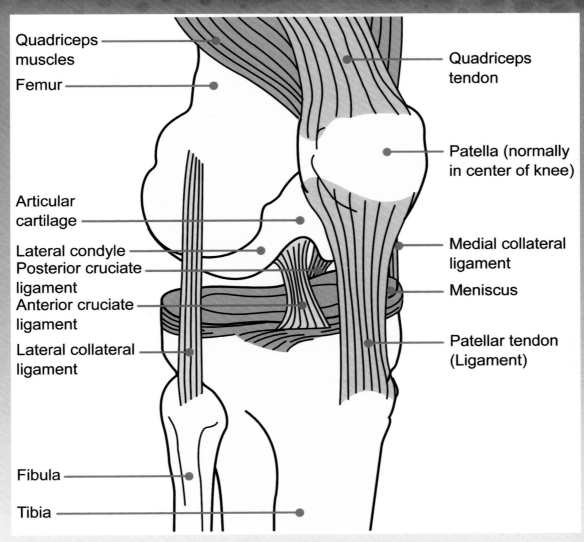

Quadriceps muscles

Femur

Articular cartilage

Lateral condyle

Posterior cruciate ligament

Anterior cruciate ligament

Lateral collateral ligament

Fibula

Tibia

Quadriceps tendon

Patella (normally in center of knee)

Medial collateral ligament

Meniscus

Patellar tendon (Ligament)

Knee injuries are not very common in volleyball, most likely because of the protective knee pads that many players wear while playing.

Repeated use of the shoulder joint to serve, bump, set, and spike the ball can result in an overuse injury, such as tendonitis. In fact, tendonitis accounts for 8–20% of all overuse injuries to the shoulder.

have shown that you are most likely to suffer if you are a jumper training hard to improve, if you bend your legs more than 90 degrees when jumping, and if you have been playing competitively for three to five years.

SHOULDERS

Shoulder tendonitis results from repeated sweeps of the arm above shoulder level and is also suffered by swimmers and tennis players. Spiking and serving are chiefly responsible for these injuries—particularly the floater serve, where the follow-through is held back, thus limiting the spin given to the ball. Symptoms include generalized pain in the shoulder area and a feeling of weakness.

LOWER BACK

A general ache at the base of the spine can result from serving and spiking. Much of the power for jump serving and spiking is generated in the lower

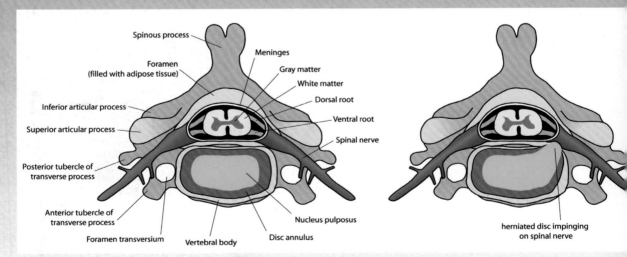

Spiking, serving, and reaching to block the ball over the net can damage the spine, causing pain in the lower back.

back, and overexertion can lead to problems. Landing also jars the lower back. Over time, these two factors may combine to cause pain.

Treatment

Any acute injury triggers a three-stage response in the body:

- First, there is damage to the tissue—muscles or ligaments—that causes bleeding. In the more severe cases, this bleeding can be seen on the surface as bruising.

- Second, the body protects the damaged area by swelling and inflaming the area. This protects the area from further impacts and prevents any movement that could increase the damage.

- Third, the body begins to repair the damage that has been done. Two to three days after the injury occurs, new blood vessels begin to form around the damaged area. Three to five days later, new tissue—a scar—is formed.

Unlike the original undamaged tissue, scar tissue needs higher maintenance to remain supple. If it is not stretched and exercised regularly, especially during the healing process, scar tissue will shrink. This leaves the damaged area greatly reduced in flexibility and prone to stiffness.

P.R.I.C.E.

Protection

As soon as you feel an injury or any unexplained pain, you need to stop playing and get off the court as quickly as possible. Move to a place or position where you can take pressure off the injury.

Rest

Let the pain settle before gently testing the injury. Can you move the joint without severe pain? If you can, keep manipulating the joint gently without causing yourself too much pain—keeping it flexible will help the healing process. If you cannot, keep the joint stationary because you will increase the damage by moving it. If the pain is especially bad, you will need to rest the joint completely for up to twenty-four hours.

Ice

Apply ice to the injury as soon as you can. This reduces inflammation, dulls the pain, and limits the damage to the soft tissue. Crushed ice should be placed in a plastic bag, then wrapped in a towel and wrapped around the injury. Applying ice directly can burn the skin. You can also use a bag of frozen peas wrapped in a towel. Apply ice for no longer than fifteen minutes. If the treatment is becoming painful, stop using ice therapy and use cold therapy instead.

Cold therapy is used for older and younger patients, whose skin is too fragile for ice therapy. Place

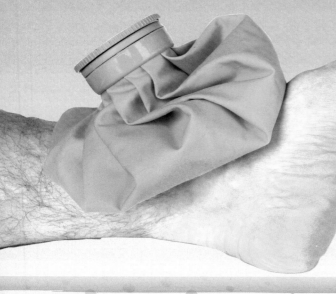

Placing ice directly on an injury can be harmful to the skin. Put the ice into a bag to eliminate this risk.

small towels in a bucket of iced water, wring one out, and wrap it around the injury. Replace with a cold towel when the first towel warms up. You can also place hands or feet in the bucket, but check on them as above. Repeat ice or cold therapy every three hours. It is particularly effective after you have been exercising.

Compression

Using a compression bandage to apply pressure to the injury will limit internal bleeding and swelling. Apply the bandage as soon as possible after the injury, but only after you have completed your first session of ice therapy. Make sure that the bandage provides pressure both above and below the injury area and is tight enough to be effective, but not so tight that it keeps blood from circulating.

Elevation

As soon as possible after the injury has been incurred, raise the injured area higher than your heart. This is done in order to limit

Wrapping an injured part of your body in elastic bandages can be a good way to allow it to heal.

bruising and swelling. Elevation should be employed as often as possible and can be combined with ice therapy or compression.

Training to Avoid Injury

Prevention is always better than cure. There is much you can do to protect yourself from acute injuries. Think about the injuries you have had and how they happened. Then plan your training schedule to address the areas in which you are weak.

Overuse injuries are very easily avoided—stop training. You may not have to stay off the court completely, though. Studies have shown that jumpers suffer the most overuse injuries, so the recommended course of action is simple: jump less! Working hard on jumping training makes little difference to the height you can reach or the power you develop. Good jumpers are good jumpers whether they train or not. If you train hard most days and feel your knees, shoulders, and lower back aching, you might consider changing games for a time, and play beach volleyball instead. You will still be enhancing your skills, but, statistically, you will be five times less likely to suffer injuries because sand is much more forgiving than a hard court.

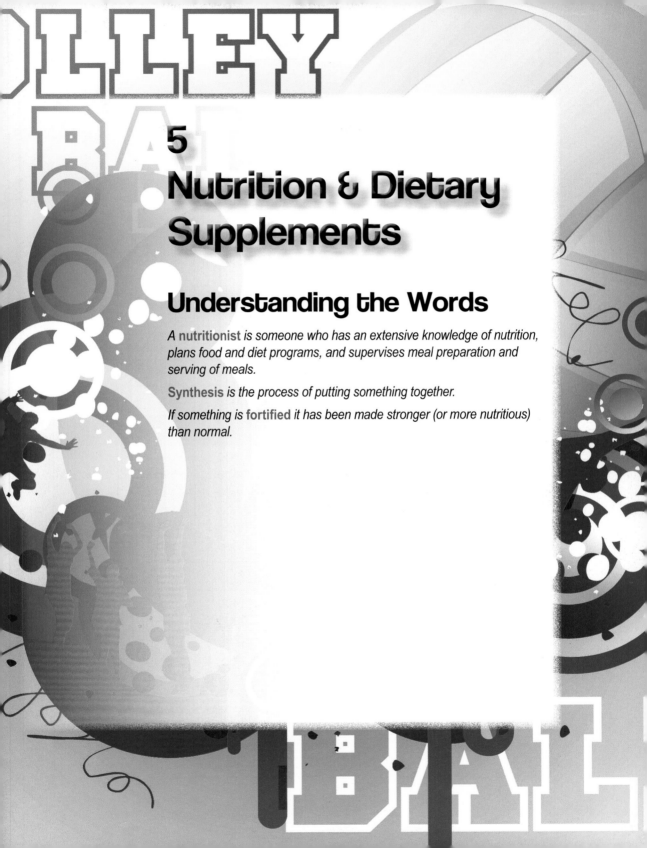

5
Nutrition & Dietary Supplements

Understanding the Words

A nutritionist *is someone who has an extensive knowledge of nutrition, plans food and diet programs, and supervises meal preparation and serving of meals.*

Synthesis *is the process of putting something together.*

If something is fortified *it has been made stronger (or more nutritious) than normal.*

Although practice and training are an important part of being safe in volleyball, it is also important to pay attention to what foods you are consuming, Athletes must be careful to eat a proper blend of nutrients to make sure their bodies and minds perform as well as they possibly can. This doesn't just mean eating healthy foods, but also choosing when to eat, how much to eat, and whether to take dietary supplements. Of course, when you choose a new diet or supplement, you should consult with a nutritionist, doctor, or some other expert. Don't make up your own nutrition program!

What to Eat

While a balanced diet is important for everyone, it is even more important for athletes. Typically, an athlete has to eat considerably more than other people do in order to maintain higher energy levels. The United States Food and Drug Administration (FDA) suggests that the average American should eat about 2,000 calories a day; for a male high school-or college-level athlete, a 3,000–4,000 calorie diet is more common. There are three main food groups to consider when choosing a diet: carbohydrates, protein, and fats.

	Calorie Range		
Children	**Sedentary** ⟶		**Active**
2–3 years	1,000	⟶	1,400
Females			
4–8 years	1,200	⟶	1,800
9–13	1,600	⟶	2,200
14–18	1,800	⟶	2,400
19–30	2,000	⟶	2,400
31–50	1,800	⟶	2,200
51+	1,600	⟶	2,200
Males			
4–8 years	1,400	⟶	2,000
9–13	1,800	⟶	2,600
14–18	2,200	⟶	3,200
19–30	2,400	⟶	3,000
31–50	2,200	⟶	3,000
51+	2,000	⟶	2,800

The number of calories you need depends partly on your level of activity.

CARBOHYDRATES

Carbohydrates are foods rich in a chemical called starch, which is what the body breaks down to get energy. Starchy foods include breads and grains, cereal, pasta, rice, and vegetables such as potatoes. Roughly half an athlete's calories should come from carbohydrates, but you should be aware of heavily processed carbohydrates such as sugary foods and white bread made with bleached flour. These foods are quickly broken down into sugars, which the body processes into fats if it does not immediately burn them off. The best

Pasta is high in carbohydrates. Whole grain pasta is a better source of complex carbohydrates than pastas made with white flour.

Cholesterol

A lot of bad things have been said about cholesterol—but most of this bad press focuses on LDLs, or low-density lipoproteins, a kind of cholesterol that can clog our blood vessels and make our heart work harder. Our bodies make this cholesterol out of saturated fats, like those found in animal fat from meats, butter, and whole milk. It is important to know, though, that there is a kind of cholesterol that has a good effect on the body. HDLs, or high-density lipoproteins can be increased as easily as exercising regularly.

carbohydrate choices for an athlete are pasta and whole-grain foods, as well as starchy vegetables, which have vitamins as well as carbohydrates. A balanced diet avoids the "empty calories" supplied by white bread and sugars.

PROTEINS

Proteins are important chemicals found in all living things; these chemicals are used to perform specific functions inside our body cells. Each protein is a long, folded chain-like molecule made up of "links" called amino acids. Our bodies can break down proteins into their base amino acids and use them to build new proteins that make up our muscles and bones. For this reason, it is important to eat enough protein to give the body the building blocks it needs to become stronger, especially during exercise. The best sources of protein are meat and dairy products such as milk or cheese, as well as eggs and certain vegetables (like soy, beans, and rice). To know how much protein to eat, a good rule of thumb is the number of grams should be equal to about one-third of your body weight in pounds. For example, a 200-pound person should have roughly 70 grams of protein per day.

FATS

Lots of times we think of fats as strictly "bad," since eating too much of them is unhealthy. However, fat is an important ingredient needed to make our bodies function correctly. Without fats, we could not absorb certain vitamins efficiently. Our skin and hair also need some amount of fat in order to grow correctly. However, fats should still be eaten in moderation—no more than 70 grams per day. The best sources of fat are vegetable oils, olive oil, and nuts. Many foods contain saturated fats, which lead to the formation of cholesterol and can force your heart to work harder.

Dietary Supplements

Many athletes seek to improve their performance by taking dietary supplements, which are pills or drinks that contain nutrients or chemicals. Dietary supplements do not include illegal performance-enhancing drugs. Instead, they contain vitamins, minerals, or chemicals that help the body use those vitamins more efficiently. When properly used, supplements can improve overall health and performance, but you should always consult a

Checking the nutrition labels on food products is the best way to know what you're taking into your body, including how much fat per serving is in a specific item.

doctor or nutritionist before taking them. Some examples of common supplements include vitamin tablets, creatine, and protein shakes or powder.

VITAMIN TABLETS

We do not always get the vitamins and nutrients we need, usually because our diets are not as balanced as they should be. Sometimes, it's because the foods available to us have been processed in such a way that they lose their nutrients. Also, exhausted soil all over the country means that fruits and vegetables are often not as nutrient-rich as they should be. In many cases, we can get vitamins we need from vitamin supplements. These supplements, usually taken as pills, contain a balanced mixture of vitamins and nutrients known as multivitamins. Sometimes they contain a single vitamin or mineral

Staying Hydrated

The best diet in the world is no good if you become dehydrated. Dehydration occurs when your body doesn't have enough water, leading to fatigue, dizziness, and headaches, all of which can hurt your performance when playing. It's best to carry a bottle of water with you the whole day before a practice or game to make sure you are fully hydrated. In addition, you should be drinking water throughout the game to avoid becoming dehydrated as you sweat. Staying fully hydrated has many benefits. Besides helping your performance in a game, it can help concentration, improve digestive health, and reduce the risk of kidney stones.

that our diet is lacking. Be careful when taking vitamin supplements, however, because it is possible to overdose on certain ones. Don't assume that more is always better! And don't forget to always talk to your doctor before beginning supplements of any kind.

CREATINE

Creatine is a specific protein naturally found in your body's muscle cells. When taken in larger doses than is found in the body, creatine has the effect

Drinking water before, during, and after physical activity is the best way to make sure your performance is not affected negatively by dehydration.

Volleyball and Alcohol

After a big victory, teammates may be tempted to celebrate with alcohol. They may also be tempted to use it to ease the pain of defeat. But alcohol intake can interfere with the body's recovery process, and this may interfere with your next game's performance.

It is especially important to avoid any alcohol 24 hours after exercise if you have any soft tissue injuries or bruises. Alcohol and injuries are a bad combination, as alcohol can actually increase swelling and bleeding, delaying the healing process.

of increasing the rate of protein synthesis within your body's cells. You will have more energy to exercise and will see a greater improvement in strength and speed when you do. However, putting any chemical into your body can have negative effects, and you should talk to a doctor before starting creatine. Creatine is only suited for adult athletes, though, so young people under the age of 17 should not take it.

PROTEIN SUPPLEMENTS

Getting enough protein from the food you eat can be difficult. Eating protein immediately after a workout is actually recommended in order to refuel your body. The problem is, not many people feel up to preparing a meal right after exercising, so protein shakes are often a convenient and healthy choice. Many shakes contain blends of protein, carbohydrates, and fats, and

Though protein shakes can be a good way to get high amounts of protein into your diet, make sure not to replace whole meals with any kind of diet supplement, including shakes.

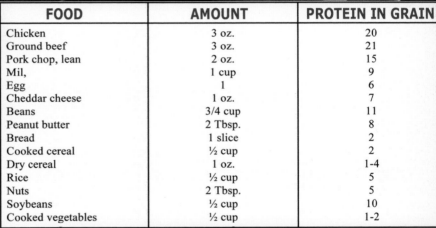

FOOD	AMOUNT	PROTEIN IN GRAIN
Chicken	3 oz.	20
Ground beef	3 oz.	21
Pork chop, lean	2 oz.	15
Mil,	1 cup	9
Egg	1	6
Cheddar cheese	1 oz.	7
Beans	3/4 cup	11
Peanut butter	2 Tbsp.	8
Bread	1 slice	2
Cooked cereal	½ cup	2
Dry cereal	1 oz.	1-4
Rice	½ cup	5
Nuts	2 Tbsp.	5
Soybeans	½ cup	10
Cooked vegetables	½ cup	1-2

Misty May-Treanor (1977-)

Legendary Olympic volleyball player Misty May-Treanor is known as one of the greatest volleyball players of all time. Born in Los Angeles, California, Misty played college volleyball at Long Beach State in her home state. While in college, she competed in the 1998 NCAA Championship and was awarded the Co-MVP award. In addition, she earned several other Athlete-of-the-Year awards, and was an NCAA First-Team All-American from 1996–1998. In 1998, her college volleyball team was one of three teams in the whole country to go undefeated that season.

Since then, she has become a legend in her sport. With her partner Kerri Walsh, also a record-breaking player, she has surpassed landmarks in the Association of Volleyball Professionals (AVP) and Olympics that have never been accom-

some include vitamins to help balance an athlete's diet. Furthermore, having protein immediately after a workout can help repair the damage sustained by your muscles during exercise. You should always remember that while protein shakes are useful for supplementing your diet, they should never be used to replace meals in significant quantities. Your body still needs plenty of

plished by women. She and Walsh have been named AVP Team of the Year four years in a row (2003–2006), and Misty was named Most Valuable Player in 2005 and 2006, Best Offensive Player in 2004–2006, and Best Defensive Player in 2006. The pair went on a record-breaking 89-match winning streak in the 2003–2004 season, and won 50 straight matches ending in July 2005.

In addition to Misty's other accomplishments in volleyball, she has competed in three summer Olympic Games: Sydney in 2000, Athens in 2004, and Beijing in 2008. In 2004 and 2008, she and Walsh won the gold, defeating both the Brazilian and Chinese teams, respectively. In 2008, Treanor was named the Most Outstanding Player for the women's competition.

nutrients that it can only get from a balanced diet. No matter how fortified a protein shake may be, it cannot adequately replace a real meal. A nutritionist can tell you how to fit protein or supplement shakes into your diet safely and effectively.

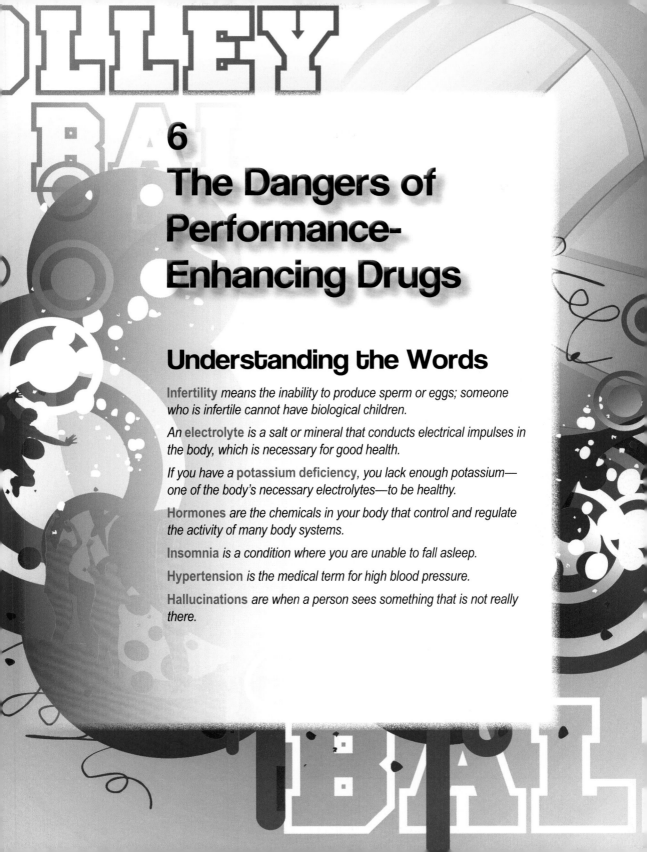

6
The Dangers of Performance-Enhancing Drugs

Understanding the Words

Infertility *means the inability to produce sperm or eggs; someone who is infertile cannot have biological children.*

An **electrolyte** *is a salt or mineral that conducts electrical impulses in the body, which is necessary for good health.*

If you have a **potassium deficiency,** *you lack enough potassium—one of the body's necessary electrolytes—to be healthy.*

Hormones *are the chemicals in your body that control and regulate the activity of many body systems.*

Insomnia *is a condition where you are unable to fall asleep.*

Hypertension *is the medical term for high blood pressure.*

Hallucinations *are when a person sees something that is not really there.*

Although volleyball is a world-renowned sport and popular all over the globe, there are still dangerous aspects that all players should be cautious of, whether in high school, college, or especially playing for a professional team. In most college or pro sports, players may encounter the temptation to use "performance-enhancing drugs," or steroids.

By definition, these "drugs" are any form of chemicals that are taken in order to improve physical strength; and while this may seem like a simple, fool-proof way to get ahead on the court—indoor or outdoor—it is

Performance-enhancing drugs usually only help you in the short term, but they will damage your body over prolonged periods of use. Training and practice are far healthier ways to get an edge over the competition, no matter the sport.

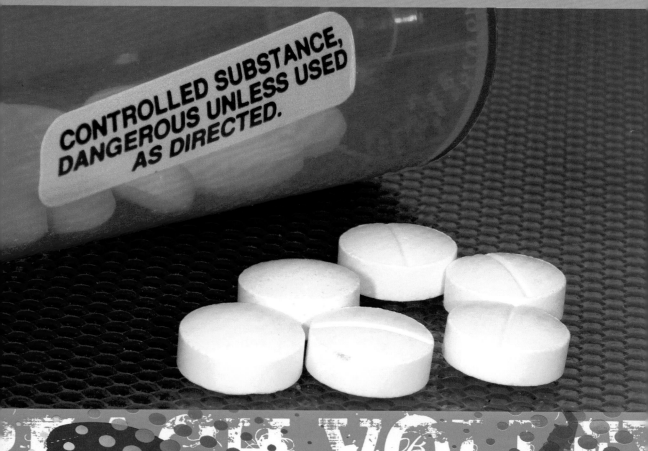

much more complicated than that. Not only are there legal consequences for getting involved with steroids but very serious health issues can also arise.

Ben Johnson, Canadian Olympian; Barry Bonds of the San Francisco Giants; and Floyd Landis, winner of the 2006 Tour de France, are all amazingly accomplished athletes—but that's not all they have in common. All their careers have been tarnished by their use of performance-enhancing drugs. Landis, for example, had his title stripped from him and was dismissed from his cycling team after a urine test came back positive for high amounts of testosterone. Johnson, who won the 1987 World Championships and 1988 Summer Olympics, had his gold medal ripped from him just days after winning because he tested positive for anabolic steroids. And Bonds was indicted by the federal grand jury and charged with supplying steroids to other athletes; even though he has 7 MVP awards and is known as one of the best major league baseball players ever, he has said that no team will pick him up now for even a minimum salary.

Although steroid use has not been very common in volleyball, there have been accusations in professional tournaments, which have led to players withdrawing and being suspended.

Anabolic-Androgenic Steroids

Anabolic-androgenic steroids are usually taken to increase muscle mass. The main natural steroid produced by the body is testosterone, which causes muscle mass and male secondary characteristics such as facial hair. Athletes take steroids such as methyl testosterone and oxymethelone in order to build muscle and recover from workouts. Since these drugs are illegal for athletes to use, beginning in 2002, "designer" drugs such as tetrahydrogestrinone (THG) have been created that allow athletes to be tested for steroid use without registering positive.

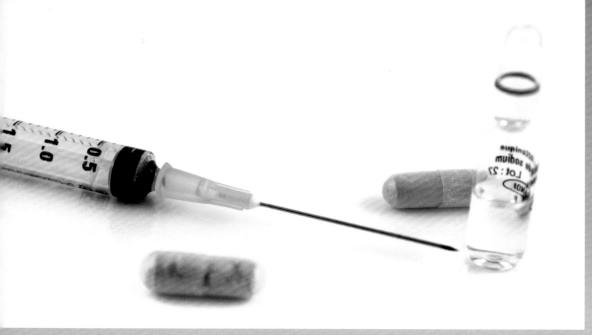

USA Volleyball works as part of the U.S. Anti-Doping Agency to promote healthy competition without the use of banned, often illegal, performance-enhancing drugs.

Many of these drugs are so new that they have not been tested thoroughly. Early indications are that these steroids may have serious side effects in men can range from baldness to breast growth, shrunken testicles, and infertility. Women tend to develop increased body hair, a deeper voice, and baldness. Both men and women may develop severe acne, liver abnormalities and tumors, cholesterol abnormalities, aggressive behavior, drug dependence, and future health risks. As of today, taking anabolic-androgenic steroids is illegal for enhancing sports performance, and they are outlawed in competition.

Diuretics

Diuretics are a class of drugs that increase urine production. Some athletes also believe that diuretics help them pass drug testing, since they dilute their urine. However, taking diuretics can upset the body's electrolyte balance and lead to dehydration. Taking diuretics such as Acetazolamide (Diamox) can lead to muscle cramps, exhaustion, dizziness, potassium deficiency, a drop in blood pressure, and even death.

Androstenedione

Androstenedione is a hormone produced naturally by the adrenal glands, ovaries, and testes, which is then converted to testosterone and estadiol, the human sex hormones. Artificially produced androstenedione is a controlled substance that is illegal in competition in the United States, though it is still being sold.

Scientific evidence suggests that androstenodione doesn't promote muscle growth, and has several risks. In men, side effects include acne, diminished sperm production, shrunken testicles, and enlargement of breasts. In women, the drug causes acne and masculinization, such as growth of facial hair. Androstenedione has also been shown to increase the chances of a heart attack and stroke because it causes the buildup of bad cholesterol.

Stimulants

Stimulants are a class of drugs that increase breathing rate, heart rate, and blood circulation. Athletes believe that these drugs stimulate their central nervous system, allowing them to perform better. Stimulants such as caffeine, cold remedies, and street drugs (cocaine and methamphetamine) can promote alertness, suppress appetite, and increase aggressiveness. However, these drugs can also make an athlete have difficulty concentrating, as well as insomnia, nervousness, and irritability. Athletes can even become psychologically addicted. Other side effects include weight loss, tremors, heart rate abnormalities, hypertension, hallucinations, and heart attacks.

Over-the-Counter Drugs

Besides these dangerous and often illegal drugs, athletes also use painkillers and sedatives to enhance their performance. Painkillers allow athletes to operate with a higher level of pain tolerance, while sedatives allow them to concentrate under stressful situations. However, these drugs can also decrease performance—and they can disqualify an athlete from competing if they are detected in his bloodstream.

The Consequences of Performance-Enhancing Drug Use

Volleyball players, like all athletes, are often looking for a greater competitive edge to gain fame, acclaim, or an award or prize. However, there is no magical concoction that will automatically bring these rewards. Instead, these performance-enhancing drugs tend to have many adverse side effects that could harm the body and its performance more than they help.

USA Volleyball is part of both the United States Anti-Doping Agency and the World Anti-Doping Agency (the USADA and WADA.) This group works with a number of national sports organizations to keep play fair for all athletes, and ensure a safe environment. The USADA works with USA Volleyball in drug testing, drug education, and teaching healthy lifestyles. In addition to drug testing, the USADA's mission is to bring awareness of the "drug industry" to coaches and athletes, since many drugs are sold as "legal performance enhancers" in nutrition stores and online.

What Professionals Have to Say About Steroids

"Steroids are for guys who want to cheat opponents."
—Lawrence Taylor

"Potential steroid users are seduced by the fake picture of health and vitality and virility. The picture doesn't show the strain on the arteries, the wear and tear on the heart and the psyche."
—Jeff Rutstein

"Certainly, as someone who is in a position to influence young people, I want to make my position very clear. I am absolutely against the use of these dangerous and illegal substances."
—Arnold Schwarzenegger

The CEO of the USADA, Travis Tygart, explains that what's "most alarming about this frightening trend is that the average consumer of today is likely taking these products under the misconception that they are improving their health, when in fact they may be putting themselves in serious jeopardy." Always consult with your doctor, coach, or nutritionist before you begin taking any dietary supplements—without knowing all the facts, you could be endangering your body.

Further Reading

Gamble, Paul. *Strength and Conditioning for Team Sports: Sport-Specific Physical Preparation for High Performance*. New York: Routledge, 2010.

Kenny, Bonnie, and Cindy Gregory. *Volleyball: Steps to Success*. Champaign, Ill.: Human Kinetics, 2006.

Price, Robert. *The Ultimate Guide to Weight Training for Volleyball*. Sportsworkout.com, 2006.

Scates, Al, and Michael Linn. *Complete Conditioning for Volleyball*. Champaign, Ill.: Human Kinetics, 2003.

Swope, Bob. *Youth Volleyball Drills, Plays, and Games Handbook*. St. Louis, Mo.: Jacobob Press LLC, 2009.

USA Volleyball. *Volleyball Systems & Strategies*. Champaign, Ill.: Human Kinetics, 2009.

Voight, Mike and Mick Haley. *Mental Toughness Training for Volleyball: Maximizing Technical and Mental Mechanics.* Monterey, Calif.: Coaches Choice, 2005.

Find Out More on the Internet

American Academy of Orthopaedic Surgeons
orthoinfo.aaos.org/topic.cfm?topic=A00177

Fédération International de Volleyball
www.fivb.ch

Sports Fitness Advisor
www.sport-fitness-advisor.com/volleyball-training.html

Sports Injury Clinic
www.sportsinjuryclinic.net

Training for Volleyball
www.trainingforvolleyball.com

USA Volleyball
usavolleyball.org

Volleyball.com
www.volleyball.com

Disclaimer

The websites listed on this page were active at the time of publication. The publisher is not responsible for websites that have changed their address or discontinued operation since the date of publication. The publisher will review and update the websites upon each reprint.

Bibliography

Beach Volleyball Database. "Misty May-Treanor," www.bvbinfo.com/player. asp?ID=1256 (14 April 2010).

ExRx. "Push Press," www.exrx.net/WeightExercises/OlympicLifts/Push-Press.html (7 April 2010).

Finest Quotes. "Steroids Quotes," www.finestquotes.com/select_quote-category-Steroids-page-0.htm (15 April 2010).

How to Deadlift with Proper Technique," stronglifts.com/how-to-deadlift-with-proper-technique/ (5 April 2010).

Inspirational Quotes and Quotations. "Top 10 List—Volleyball Motivational Quotes," www.inspirational-quotes-and-quotations.com/volleyball-motiva-tional-quotes.html (14 April 2010).

MedicineNet.com. "Definition of Meditation," www.medterms.com/script/main/art.asp?articlekey=10807 (5 April 2010).

Peak Performance. "Upper body exercises: Straight arm pullover," www.pponline.co.uk/encyc/upper-body-exercises-straight-arm-pullover-3 (5 April 2010).

Running Planet. "Running Specific Strength Training Exercises," www.run-ningplanet.com/training/running-specific-strength.html (5 April 2010).

Sports Fitness Advisor. "Volleyball Plyometrics Program," www.sport-fitness-advisor.com/volleyball-plyometrics.html (7 April 2010).

Sports Injury Clinic. "Strapping and Taping," www.sportsinjuryclinic.net/strapping-and-taping.php#role (5 April 2010).

Strength and Power for Volleyball. "Motivational Volleyball Quotes," www.strength-and-power-for-volleyball.com/volleyball-quotes-team.html (14 April 2010).

Strength and Power for Volleyball. "Volleyball Fitness," www.strength-and-power-for-volleyball.com/volleyball-fitness.html (7 April 2010).

Top Tenz. "Top 10 Sports Figures Whose Careers are Tarnished by Steroids," www.toptenz.net/top-10-sports-figures-steroids.php (15 April 2010).

Volleyball Advisors. "Volleyball Quotes and Sayings for Inspiration," www.volleyballadvisors.com/volleyball-quotes.html (14 April 2010).

Volleyball Advisors. "Volleyball Workout—Strength Training Basics," www.volleyballadvisors.com/volleyball-workout.html (7 April 2010).

Index

Picture Credits

Choy, Andrew; Creative Commons: p. 35
Creative Commons: p. 18
Jenkins, Suzanne; USAF: p. 53
Martin, David: Creative Commons: p. 11
U.S. Army: p. 36
Wikimedia Foundation: p. 54
Wronowski, Grzegorz; Creative Commons: p. 51

To the best knowledge of the publisher, all images not specifically credited are in the public domain. If any image has been inadvertently uncredited, please notify Harding House Publishing Service, 220 Front Street, Vestal, New York 13850, so that credit can be given in future printings.

About the Author and the Consultants

Gabrielle Vanderhoof is a former competitive figure skater who hopes to have a career in publishing public relations. This is her first time writing for Mason Crest.

Susan Saliba, Ph.D., is a senior associate athletic trainer and a clinical instructor at the University of Virginia in Charlottesville, Virginia. A certified athletic trainer and licensed physical therapist, Dr. Saliba provides sports medicine care, including prevention, treatment, and rehabilitation for the varsity athletes at the university. Dr. Saliba is a member of the national Athletic Trainers' Association Educational Executive Committee and its Clinical Education Committee.

Eric Small, M.D., a Harvard-trained sports medicine physician, is a nationally recognized expert in the field of sports injuries, nutritional supplements, and weight management programs. He is author of *Kids & Sports* (2002) and is Assistant Clinical professor of pediatrics, Orthopedics, and Rehabilitation Medicine at Mount Sinai School of Medicine in New York. He is also Director of the Sports Medicine Center for Young Athletes at Blythedale Children's Hospital in Valhalla, New York. Dr. Small has served on the American Academy of Pediatrics Committee on Sports Medicine, where he develops national policy regarding children's medical issues and sports.